OCD: THE ERP CURE - FIVE PRINCIPLES AND FIVE STEPS TO TURN OFF OCD

By

Christian R. Komor, Psy.D.

OCD: THE ERP CURE - FIVE PRINCIPLES AND FIVE STEPS TO TURN OFF OCD

© 2012 by Christian R. Komor

All material in this course is, unless otherwise stated, the property of Dr. Christian R. Komor. Copyright and other intellectual property laws protect these materials. Reproduction or retransmission of the materials, in whole or in part, in any manner, without the prior written consent of the copyright holder, is a violation of copyright law.

A single copy of the materials available through this course may be made, solely for personal, noncommercial use. Individuals must preserve any copyright or other notices contained in or associated with them. Users may not distribute such copies to others, whether or not in electronic form, whether or not for a charge or other consideration, without prior written consent of the copyright holder of the materials. Contact information for requests for permission to reproduce or distribute materials available through this course are listed below: Christian R. Komor, Psy.D., OCD Recovery Center, P.O. Box 6654, Grand Rapids, MI 49516

Library of Congress Cataloging in Publication Data

Komor, Christian R., 1959-
 OCD: The ERP Cure – Five Principles and Five Steps to Turn Off OCD

By Christian R. Komor.
  p. cm.
 includes bibliographic references.
  1. Anxiety 2. Self-Help
I. Title.
RC569.5.WW67K66 1992
616.85'2 – dc20   92-13568

ISBN-13: 978-1478330578

ISBN-10: 1478330570

CIP

Publisher: KEI GLOBAL
             P.O. Box 6025
             Grand Rapids, Michigan 49516
             www.keiglobal.com

DEDICATION

This book is dedicated to a precious and gentle soul from California who lost his life to Body Dysmorphic Disorder. May you find the peace in your next life which eluded you in this one.

CONTENTS

Introduction..5

Chapter One: Understanding The Enemy Is The First Step To Success..7

The OCD Cycle..11

Types Of Obsessions - Common, Global, Intrusive, Pan-Obsessions..13

Chapter Two: The "Five & Five" – Beating OCD At Its Own Game By Changing The Brain!..14

The Magical ERP Genie Exercise..20

Chapter Three: Some Concluding Thoughts..21

Appendix: Helpful Reminders For Difficult Times In Recovery..22

References And Readings..24

INTRODUCTION

Obsessive Compulsive Disorder is a bewildering, confusing, paradoxical, torturous, and very, very uncomfortable neurobiological disorder which can wreak havoc not just on the individual sufferer, but also on their relationships, home life, school and work. Indeed, if you do have someone with OCD in your life you are probably wondering, "How did I get into this?" or even more likely "How do I get out of this?!" You want to know how to best assist them, but don't want to get sucked into the rituals and just downright weirdness that goes with OCD. You'd like everybody to be able to go on with their lives and live happily ever after. You'd like the OCD to go away and leave everyone alone!

Obsessive Compulsive Spectrum Disorders (OCSD) including OCD, Asperger's Disorder, Tourette's Disorder, Hypochondriasis, Compulsive Hoarding, Trichotillomania, and Body Dysmorphic Disorder are chronic and often severely handicapping neuropsychological problems. Studies suggest OCD itself is in part genetically hard-wired into the brain (specifically the cortical-thalamic-striatal pathway of the basal ganglia) at birth though its activation and expression can be affected by personality factors, immune system changes, hormonal fluctuations, weather, diet and many other factors. For most patients a variety of lifestyle changes and treatment interventions are necessary in order to reduce intrusive obsessive thinking and compulsive behavior as well as heal the depression which often accompanies OCD and restore self-care, relationships and healthy lifestyle patterns

As usual there is good news and bad news. The good news is together we can make OCD significantly better so that life can go on. The bad news is that, like other neurobiological illnesses (Multiple Sclerosis, Parkinson's disease, Huntington's, etc.) OCD is a physical problem that, once activated, is generally with someone for life at some level. Unlike those other diseases and disorders, however, OCD responds very well to modifications in behavior which in turn send feedback back to the brain, which in turn assist the brain in *healing itself* from the OCD. We now know from brain imagery research that not only can behavior therapy change how the OCD brain *functions*, but it can also help the brain to *restructure itself* (e.g. grow new neurons) to work around or correct the faulty circuitry which is causing the OCD! So this is pretty good news really – but only if you know exactly how to treat the OCD. OCD treatment is very specialized and requires counter-intuitive techniques that general practice counselors do not usually have knowledge of. Like all living things the OCD has a will to survive and will resist attempts to kill it or disable it. We must be knowledgeable and clever in our efforts to fight it, or we could end up throwing gasoline on the fire and making everything worse!

As your author I not only have significant OCD myself, but have also had the privilege of working with hundreds of OCD patients in all different settings across America over a span of more than 15 years. I have also taught one-day seminars in over 100 cities for thousands of professional learning to treat OCD and Obsessive Compulsive Spectrum Disorders. This wealth of experience has allowed me to develop innovative techniques which have led to a higher success rate in achieving symptom remission. *If you were to engage in counseling with me to treat OCD the process represented in this book would be the one we would follow!*

Research has made it abundantly clear that the mind and body not only work together but cannot really even be considered as separate. As we change our thoughts we change how our brains function and when we change our metabolism, diet or neurotransmitters we change our thoughts and feelings. In fact, there are many medical conditions, medications and some supplements and vitamins which can cause a worsening of anxiety or depression. (I can provide a listing of such items upon request.). In order to rule out the possibility that the difficulties you are experiencing may have a primarily medical origin, I suggest that you ask your general physician for a physical evaluation. From my experience it is less costly and time consuming to rule out physical contributors in this way than to spend weeks or months "counseling" an under-active thyroid gland or hormone imbalance.

The mind/body healing process can often be a demanding one. In general, I have found that the more a person is willing to be open and to take risks, make changes, and not give up on themselves the more they are likely to grow. Frequently, the process involves both (1) an emotional journey into our personal origins and (2) the learning of present-day skills for living in harmony with our self and our world. During the healing process you may find yourself: releasing and "metabolizing" blocked feelings; developing and integrating new insights; learning healthy self-care behaviors; and developing new experiential pathways. I generally have observed that 25% of our work together is in discovering "what needs doing" and 75% in making action plans and putting those into effect.

It is important to remember that mind/body healthcare continues outside the consulting office. Following through on suggested personal growth activities outside of session is crucial to the success of your therapy. I highly encourage you to keep a journal or notebook to help in recording insights, feelings and questions that come to you during, as well as between, our meetings. For optimal use of this medium I suggest dividing the notebook into two parts - *Process* (e.g. feelings, questions, concerns) and *Discoveries* (e.g. insights, affirmations, self-care solutions).

CHAPTER ONE: UNDERSTANDING THE ENEMY IS THE FIRST STEP TO SUCCESS

The purpose of this chapter is to give you a little scientific overview of Obsessive Compulsive Disorder and what makes it tick. As long as we feel that our obsessions are "real" and must therefore be obeyed we are lost. We must be able to stand back from them, detach and look at them objectively. In other words we must see them for what they truly are – error messages from our brain. To do this we must first understand the nature of OCD, where it comes from and what it is up to. Let's start with defining some terms we will be using.

> **Obsession**: Recurrent, persistent unwanted thoughts, impulses, or images that are difficult to shake off and experienced as intrusive and inappropriate causing marked anxiety or distress. (Types: Common, Global, Intrusive)

> **Neutralization**: The performance of a behavior, ritual, compulsive action or thought in order to reduce anxiety of psychic discomfort.

> **Compulsion / Ritual**: Repetitive behaviors or mental acts that the person feels driven to perform in response to anxiety and or obsession

> **Over-Valued Ideation**: Unreasonable belief or idea not held as firmly as a delusion. Person is able to acknowledge possibility the belief may not be true.

> **Delusion**: False belief based on incorrect inference about external reality despite what constitutes incontrovertible proof or evidence to the contrary.

> **Thought Fusion**: OCD is highly associational, meaning that it will create links in the person's mind between things that do not really have any association with each other (e.g. "Because I think about a cemetery I am going to die today") Thought fusion can take several forms: (1) Cognition that thinking something is as bad as doing it. This is called *moral thought action fusion*. (2) Cognition that thinking about something will make them do it, this is *thought action fusion*. (3) Cognition that thinking about something happening changes the probability of something happening. This is *thought event fusion*. (4) Cognition that thinking something can lead to thought attaching to an object which is *thought object fusion*.

Obsessive Compulsive Disorder itself is classified in the Diagnostic and Statistical Manual of Mental Disorders as an Anxiety Disorder. To diagnose OCD one must have (1) Obsessions and (2) Compulsions that cause (3) Distress over 1 hour per day. OCD affects somewhere around 3% of the population and in seen at roughly the same prevalence in all cultures around the world. Generally the onset of OCD occurs prior to age 18 and begins a slowly worsening course across the lifespan. Major life events or physiological changes (childbirth, menopause, trauma) can cause the OCD to worsen or sometimes improve.

The World Health Organization lists OCD is among the top ten causes of disability worldwide and OCD is among top three most disabling psychological disorders along with Schizophrenia & Bipolar Disorders. OCD is twice a prevalent as Schizophrenia and Bipolar Disorders. In the USA alone the medical costs of OCD are estimated to be 2-5 billion dollars annually with lost productivity costs over 6 billion.

OCD can severely impact an individual's quality of life. We know from catchment studies that:

- **75% of OCD patients experience significant depression.**
- **73% of OCD patients have impaired family relationships.**
- **58% are without a primary family unit.**
- **62% report impaired friendships.**
- **58% report academic underachievement.**
- **47% report interference with work.**
- **40% are chronically unemployed or underemployed.**

In general statistics show people with OCD having levels of quality of life lower than chronic medical conditions as a group.

The most *detailed definition* of OCD is as follows: "OCD is a highly comorbid, genetically loaded, neuro-psychological disability commonly influenced by immunological and, or hormonal events resulting in cognitive and affective dysfunction with a wide range of behavioral manifestations."

We will talk about some of the elements underlined above, but first let us digress to note that OCD can strike anyone at any age in any walk of life. It is not related to a person's character or morality and bears no reflection on their overall intelligence.

Many famous people have had OCD and yet contributed greatly to society (or at least gotten themselves famous) including:

- Jeremy Lyons - Actor
- Howie Mandel – Unknown purpose
- Kathie Lee Gifford - Wow!
- Dr. Samuel Johnson - Did Something Significant
- Donald Trump - Famous hair model
- Cameron Diaz - Famous hair model
- Mariette Hartley - Actress
- Eric Bernotas - Olympic crazy-person
- Nikola Tesla - Science buff
- Alec Baldwin - Actor
- Michael Jackson – Deceased alien life-form
- Howard Hughes - Very rich person

- Denise Richards – Not married to Keith Richards
- Adrian Monk – Not a real person

Having worked with hundreds of OCD patients of all types and trained several thousand professionals in optimal methods of treating OCD I can tell you from experience that OCD is a powerful force to be reckoned with. Yes, there are folks out there who have "just a little OCD" which is not too bothersome, or easily put in its place. In the main, however, people seeking treatment for OCD are among the most tormented individuals on the planet – at least in their own thoughts. Outwardly life may be going great, but inside the individual the fears involved when a person has OCD can OCD can be stronger than even the human survival instinct! In speaking with veterans who have OCD it is clear that a short circuiting brain can generate more fear than armed combat! Moreover, OCD recovery rates are only slightly better than Schizophrenia - around 33% achieved long-lasting symptomatic remission during a 3 year follow-up period. OCD recovery rates are also lower than for Bipolar I Disorder where around 47% of patients survived without a mood episode during a 1-year of follow-up. Around 9% - 14% of folks with OCD experience a slow deteriorating course regardless of intervention. Here are some more sobering statistics:

When treated with optimum cognitive-behavioral therapy:
- 20% withdraw from CBT.
- 20-30% "unresponsive" to CBT.
- In responders, 43-68% have symptoms at follow-up.
- Only 11% fully asymptomatic at follow-up.

When treated with optimum medication:
- 47% drop out rate due to side effects 12% complete remission.
- 47% partial remission.
- Significant relapse rate in responders.
- 20% unable to "reuse" medication after initial success.
- Average 30% treatment effect in 60% of patients (minus placebo).

PLEASE DO NOT MAKE THE MISTAKE OF UNDERESTIMATING THE POWER OF OCD. In severe situations the OCD will literally kill the individual if it gets the chance. I have personally worked with many situations where either the OCD was close to killing the patient and a handful in which we were too late to intervene and it did. This will usually happen in one or more of three ways: (1) The OCD will make the individual so depressed and hopeless that they take their own life, (2) The OCD will cut off so many self-care abilities and resources that the person cannot sustain life (e.g. not being able to eat or drink), (3) Creating "dares" and "challenges" that end in death (e.g. having to perform risky driving maneuvers). So our enemy is powerful and cunning and in response we must be vigilant, clever, decisive and energetic in our strategies to defeat it. To do that we must first understand our enemy thoroughly.

When we look closely the experience of someone with OCD we see that they are typically plagued with several different "problems" each of which by themselves could easily give anyone a really bad day! Together they combine to create a truly nasty cocktail:

These elements interact in what is termed the "OCD Cycle" which can be seen in almost every individual with this OCD. The OCD Cycle is illustrated on the following page.

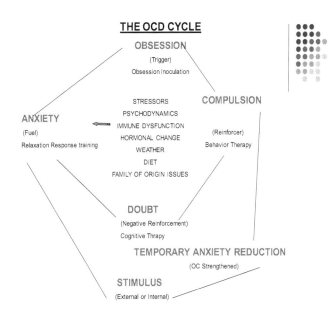

Capitalized in the chart are the main elements of the "OCD Cycle". OCD can be said to "begin" with a large pool of anxiety which follows the individual throughout their day. When the individual runs into a "STIMULUS" or trigger for their particular OBSESSION the cortical-thalamic-striatal pathway in the basal ganglia region of the brain will become active. AT this point the individual's awareness will be shifted inward as their mind moves to examine more closely the obsessive thought and attempt to resolve it. This process will lead to the stimulation of a COMPULSION or RITUAL which the OCD tells the individual will keep them safe from the danger presented in the obsession. Performance of the COMPULSION will usually lead to a temporary reduction in anxiety which then reinforces the ritual and makes it more likely that the person will perform the ritual again when confronted with the same or similar stimulus. Unfortunately, the individual will then have added to their ANXIETY POOL since they never know when the dangerous OBSESSION will be stimulated again and if they will be able to perform the "need" COMPULSION correctly to eliminate the danger as they did this time. Thus the OCD Cycle continues to feed on itself.

In the center of the chart you will notice examples of variables which can energize or de-energize the OCD Cycle. They do not create the cycle, but can cause it to worsen or improve depending on the situation.

In small print below each of the capitalized elements of the OCD cycle you will see one or more interventions which can be applied at that particular point in the cycle. For our purposes here we will be discussing "Behavior Therapy" and "Cognitive Therapy" which can be effectively combined to create Cognitive Behavioral Therapy (or CBT) and more specifically **Exposure and Response Prevention CBT.**

As we will see, all evidence points to OCD as being a genetically determined brain dysfunction. Therefore the OCD Cycle can be thought of as "hard-wired" into the brain at birth. While OCD may or may not become active as a particular person grows into adulthood, the disorder is still there – like a balloon is still a balloon even if there is no air in it to make it visible to others.

TYPES OF OBSESSIONS - COMMON, GLOBAL, INTRUSIVE, PAN-OBSESSIONS

There are several different types of obsessions which you might encounter – even sometimes within the same individual!

Common Obsessions

- ❖ Obsessive thoughts which are connected to immediate life circumstances and events.
- ❖ Cause discomfort, but usually not disability.
- ❖ Examples:
  - "Do I love her? What is love anyway?
  - Making sure things are in certain places
  - Must have exercise, or sex a certain way or eat a certain food in a certain order
  - Forcing self to do activities completely, or eat all of something
  - Lining up objects (e.g. media collections)
  - Keeping money in order

Global Obsessions

- ❖ Fully formed thoughts which many times center around anxiety-laden issues such as religion, harming others, sexuality, bodily injury. (e.g. "I might be gay.")
- ❖ Pervasive, all-consuming, life-infringing obsessions.
- ❖ Usually highly disturbing to the individual and make it difficult to function in work, relationships and self-care.
- ❖ Stalkers suffer from global relationship obsessions.

Intrusive Obsessions

- ❖ Uncommon. The mind focuses on a particular fragment of awareness such as a sound or number or aspect of color or light and becomes caught in an endless feedback loop.
- ❖ Persistent and difficult to treat.
- ❖ Give us perspective on biological nature of OCD.
- ❖ Examples:
  - Songs, noises, images
  - Phrases that replay over and over in the mind and seem impossible to shut off.

CHAPTER TWO: THE "FIVE AND FIVE" – BEATING OCD AT IT'S OWN GAME BY CHANGING THE BRAIN!

While a broad-based recovery program is essential, the core of OCD intervention remains Exposure and Response Prevention (ERP), usually conducted in the form of Cognitive Behavioral Therapy (CBT). In ERP the individual comes into *contact* with the thought, situation, person, or object they fear and remains in contact with the *feared stimulus* long enough for the brain to *habituate* to the stimulus. This is much like jumping in a cold lake of water and staying in the water long enough for the body to become accustomed to it. Without taking the risk of exposure to feared situations it is impossible for any of us with OCD to really progress in the healing process. When we do so, on the other hand, brain imagery studies have shown us there is actual functional *and structural* healing which takes place the cortical-thalamic-striatal region of the brain – something that is impossible to produce through any other method - including medication.

Success with ERP-based treatment is dependent on following a basic set of *Five Principles* (which are then put into action using the *5 Steps* which are the focus of this article).

THE 5 PRINCIPLES FOR DEVELOPING - ERP / CBT EXERCISES

I. SAFETY / TRUST – Your obsession may have A slice of the pie may be reality, but 99% is obsession and that is what we risk – which is no true risk at all. Trust!

II. INTENSITY / EXPOSURE - Identify situations where OCD presents a challenge, list from most bothersome (100pts) to least (10pts). Target items in 25-75 range. "Expose" to 1-3 items at a time keeping anxiety levels between 25-75 and creatively modifying exercise as needed.

III. NEUTRALIZATION / RESPONSE PREVENTION – (Rituals or Compulsions) Sometimes OC sufferers have been known to "hold out" for weeks or months before performing a compulsion or ritual to " make it better" and thus neutralize the ERP work.

VI. SATURATION / HABITUATION – Making the exposure constantly present –Commitment - Habituation

V. DURATION / PERSISTANCE – Holding the exposure for as long as it takes for habituation to occur and repeating the exposure. Find a way to monitor progress.

These are referred to as the *Five Principles* of ERP. We use these *Five Principles* like a recipe to design ERP exercises. When we include all five factors the exercise is almost guaranteed success!

But once we have designed an exercise using the *Five Principles* how does one negotiate a course through the sometimes confusing and usually terrifying act of turning to face one's obsessions while not succumbing to the urge to neutralize the anxiety through rituals or compulsions? Frequently OCD sufferers will report that car accidents, hurricanes, earthquakes, public speaking, near plane-crashes and even armed combat the like are not nearly as frightening as confronting an obsession! It is precisely because it is so difficult to refuse to perform obsessive-compulsive rituals in the face of the feared obsession that it is important to have a set procedure for doing so. *OCD Recovery Centers of America* have developed a specific **5 *Step procedure*** for walking through the fear of Exposure and Response Prevention. These **5 Steps**, if followed closely, will take the OC sufferer step-by-step through the flames of anxiety that can seem so intense.

It is recommended that, after making whatever modifications are needed to tailor the procedure to one's own situation, the **5 Steps** should be applied consistently day after day so that they become second nature. The steps have been given short labels to make them easier to remember them in practice.

STEP 1: SELECT TARGET AND MODIFY INTENSITY IF NEEDED
- Essentially this is what is accomplished using the *5 Principles* above
- Rituals achieving a Subjective Units of Distress (SUD) rating of 25-75 are selected. The dangers in selecting items with SUD ratings over 75 are: *Panic, refusal, neutralization, reinforcement of obsession.*
- Change choice of target.
- Change how target is experienced by:
    - Adding or removing mediators (e.g. wearing gloves).
    - Adding or subtracting anxiety reduction techniques.
    - Adding or subtracting reassurance or modeling.
    - Increasing or decreasing duration of exposure or physical distance.

Discussion: When creating an Exposure and Response Prevention exercise, or inadvertently encountering an exposure stimulus in daily life it is important to make the experience of the stimulus (e.g. the level of anxiety it generates) manageable. This may not always be possible, and it is preferable to face down a very high anxiety situation rather than avoid or ritualize it. Most OC sufferers have a variety of compulsive behaviors they perform on a daily basis. Some, if stopped, would result in very intense anxiety leading to panic, and an increase in future compulsive rituals. Others carry with them only mild anxiety and can be fairly easily eliminated without undue stress. In choosing which OC rituals to confront it is wise to make a list of all rituals and then rate them from highest ("100") to lowest ("0") in terms of the anxiety that would be generated if the behavior were stopped. Then rituals achieving a rating of 25-75 are selected for ERP.

Sometimes it may be necessary to modify the strength of the stimulus/situation. For example, one could spend only a few minutes by a trash can instead of an hour, or wear gloves while pumping gas, or ask someone to do the behavior first. All of these are "mediators" which will titrate the exposure to a manageable range – much as medication is titrated so that the patient will not get too much or too little. This allows us to hit the "therapeutic window" at wish the exposure does the most good without overwhelming the individual.

STEP 2: SEPARATE THOUGHTS AND EXPERIENTAL AWARENESS
- Realizing that the urge to perform the obsessive ritual is in reality a faulty brain message not a real danger.
- *Stopping all activity* and concentrating one's awareness on what's happening - on the obsession or ritual - long enough to *truly and clearly see and feel* it is just OCD and not a "real" danger or issue.
- Through "bare attention"
- Develop trust in a higher power, the universe, destiny or life itself to take care of the portion of reality that may be giving rise to the obsession.

Discussion: It is crucial to note, however, that since obsessions are essentially thoughts that have gotten stuck in the individual's awareness, if we could eliminate our thoughts (or even control them) we could theoretically eliminate OCD!

In Step 2 the individual reminds him or herself that the urge to perform the obsessive ritual is in reality a faulty brain message. Usually this means actually *stopping all activity* and concentrating one's awareness on what's happening - on the obsession or ritual, long enough to *truly and clearly see and feel* it is just OCD and not a "real" danger or issue. Armed with this awareness it is then possible to be aware both mentally and experientially that the compulsion is not a real choice, but rather an expression of the obsessive compulsive disorder. Various slogans and other forms of self-talk can be used to achieve this end. It also helps, in this Step, to have a working awareness of one's mental, physical, and emotional symptoms of anxiety. This allows the patient to say, "This is just anxiety caused by the obsession or compulsion I am refusing to give in to." Usually the key is to (1) Focus awareness intensely on our awareness of our physical surroundings – separating that reality from the "fantasy world" of our thoughts

An example might be getting stuck on an obsessional thought while pulling out of the driveway. In this situation I first make the decision to practice Bare Attention. I force my awareness

---

THE 5 STEPS FOR CONDUCTING ER-ERP CBT EXERCISES

1) **SELECT** TARGET AND MODIFY INTENSITY IF NEEDED

2) **SEPARATE** THOUGHTS AND EXPERIENTAL AWARENESS

3) **IDENTIFY** THE THOUGHTS AS IRRATIONAL AND **BREAK** THE ASSOCIATIONAL CONNECTION OR "FUSION"

4) **REFUSE** TO PERFORM THE RITUAL REQUIRED BY THE OCD AND **RESIST** THE DESIRE TO NEUTRALIZE THE ANXIETY

5) **LIVE** LIFE WHILE CONTINUING TO DEVALUE THOUGHTS AND OBSERVE ANXIETY

---

into the present and even talk to myself silently, "I am pulling out of the driveway. See the neighbor's houses. Pavements looks dry. Children are playing. Turning on turn signal. Shifting to drive." For it to work we have to be very, very PRESENT, awake, alert and conscious. If we can do this, even the intrusive obsessive thoughts (much less likely to pop up during Bare Attention) appear as "just thoughts" of no more significance than the itch on my arm from yesterdays allergy shot."

As with so many things to do with OCD, the success of Bare Attention relies on brain science! There are really two directions we can turn our mind's focus – inward or outward. When we are listening to OCD we are of course focusing inward. The more we pay attention to it – trying to get all our rituals "right" the more we tune into our inner world. When we focus outside ourselves on our environment and our bodies we shift our consciousness to an entirely different area of the brain – a non-OCD area! It is this critical shift from inward to outward that brings us relief from our OCD. It literally turns off the OCD part of our brain.

Again, however, one must be cautious as Steps 2 and 4 can easily be taken over by the OCD and turned into a neutralizing compulsion. These Steps should only be used if the anxiety is so strong that it is impossible to accomplish the exercise without their assistance.

STEP 3: IDENTIFY THE THOUGHTS AS IRRATIONAL AND BREAK THE ASSOCIATIONAL CONNECTION OR "FUSION"
- Most people find some variation of asking "Would someone else have to do this? Do other people have to do this to be okay?"
-

STEP 4: REFUSE TO PERFORM THE RITUAL REQUIRED BY THE OCD AND **RESIST** THE DESIRE TO NEUTRALIZE THE ANXIETY
- A ritual is selected for elimination
- Individual refuses to perform the ritual behavior or thought in spite of the urgings of the OC disorder.
- This is done with an awareness that the surge of anxiety experienced when refusing a ritual will dissipate within minutes to hours (often in 15 to 20 minutes).

Discussion: This is the most important step in the process. People with OCD will have primary and backup rituals for relieving anxiety. They can wait for long periods of time before performing a compulsion so that they can fool themselves into believing it is not connected to the initial stimulus exposure. Neutralizing strategies can be very, very subtle such as a blink, a head shake or thinking about a color. It is *essential* to realize what neutralizing strategies are being employed and to stop them. Neutralizing strategies will always short-circuit the treatment process if allowed to continue. It is better to choose an exercise that fosters less anxiety and is manageable without performing a compulsion than choose a more difficult ERP exercise and later give in and neutralize the anxiety.

In this Step a measure of trust is often necessary. Here we are developing trust which usually means trust in a higher power, the universe, destiny or life itself. The well-know "*Serenity Prayer*" exemplifies this Step: *"Grant me the serenity to accept the things I cannot change, the courage to change the things I can and the wisdom to know the difference."* The key is in reminding oneself that compulsive rituals are designed to try to control what cannot be controlled. Yes, one may choose to brush one's teeth in order to prevent cavities, but replacing the toothbrush seven times in the toothbrush holder will not prevent AIDS. So while riding out the anxiety arising from ERP, the OC sufferer is encouraged to again and again remember to let go of what cannot and should not be controlled.

STEP 5: LIVE LIFE WHILE CONTINUING TO DEVALUE THOUGHTS, AND OBSERVE ANXIETY
- Simply allow the anxiety to be present like energy passing through the body.
- Do "anxiety checks" every 5 minutes.
- Observing the anxiety level decreasing provides strong encouragement.
- Persist in refusing the ritual until the anxiety dissipates – however long this may take.
- Once the anxiety does begin to reduce it is essential to avoid the temptation to perform another ritual to "un-do" the exposure.
- Confronting OCD leads the individual into a series of profound changes in perspective and emotions.
- Initial reaction may be increase in over-valued ideation and loss of perspective.
- Sadness, grief, pain and anger may follow.
- New realizations may occur immediately following exposure to the stimulus without the protection of rituals and compulsions.
- Write down new awareness and realizations for future reference.
- Realize it is not necessary to obsessively focus on the anxiety that is naturally generated through the exercise – just go on with life.
- Simply be aware of the anxiety.
- *Carrying the anxiety along.*

Discussion: Once a ritual is selected for elimination and we refuse to perform the ritual behavior or thought in spite of the urgings of the OCD, a surge of anxiety will be experienced. This anxiety surge will eventually dissipate within minutes to hours (often in 15 to 20 minutes). The OC sufferer is encouraged to *maintain awareness* of the anxiety by doing "*anxiety checks*" every five minutes until the anxiety has dropped by 50% from its initial **strength**. At that point the individual can go on about their daily activities without needing to maintain awareness of the anxiety. It is important to remember that anxiety may show itself in thoughts, feelings, physical reactions and, or behavior. Each individual will be unique in their pattern of anxiety reactions and it may help to identify one's specific anxiety symptoms prior to engaging in ERP.

It is necessary to persist in refusing the ritual until the anxiety dissipates – however long this may take. Like aerobic exercise, which must be done for a certain length of time in order to have cardiovascular benefits, one's anxiety level *must* have decreased by at least 50% before any positive benefits will accrue. Of course, once the anxiety has dissipated the individual will feel no need to perform the compulsive behavior! Time is a key factor in the healing process. Many people with OC disorders will refuse a ritual, but then go ahead and do it in a little while. This will only provide the OC disorder with what is known as "intermittent reinforcement" – a strong reinforcer to continue generating obsessive and compulsive demands. It helps greatly for the patient to take note of their anxiety level (0-100) every ten minutes or so along the way. Observing the anxiety level decreasing provides strong encouragement.

It is not necessary to obsessively focus on the anxiety that is naturally generated when refusing to perform a compulsive ritual. The key is to be aware of the anxiety, to see it for what it is and then do something else – go on with life *carrying the anxiety with you*. The optimal procedure is to say to one self "Yes, I am anxious because of the ritual I am refusing to perform. Now I am going to go on and do something that I *choose* to do." There is an exciting element of risk here. It can be unsettling to step out and assert one's own choices and desires after being a slave so long to the compulsive behavior.

While not always the case, often after following through successfully with an ERP exercise feelings of grief, elation, anger, etc. will arise. It is well to give these feelings some attention, allowing oneself to vent or express them with another person, listening to expressive music, or even hitting a punching bag. The idea is not to obsess on the feelings, but simply to let the flow. Sometimes this will lead to additional realizations and insights which can then be notated earlier. It is generally helpful to most people with OCD to keep a journal in which they can keep track of therapeutic recommendations and homework assignments, chart progress, notate problems with procedures, and make observations. This material can be brought back to the treatment sessions and will vastly increase the effectiveness of the treatment process.

Finally, providing oneself with some level or type of praise, reward or reinforcement for job well done certainly has an important place in the process of ERP. It is highly beneficial to find a specific way of rewarding oneself each time an obsession has been challenged.

Dr Komor's Patented ERP Gratitue Now Exercise (ERP-GNE or "ERP Genie")

This special technique for dealing with those "OCD moments" incorporates several essential elements in OCD recovery: exposure and response prevention, living in the present moment, gratitude versus scanning for danger.

All of the research to date indicates that in order to improve our situation in relation to OCD we must be willing to face the fear of "exposing" ourselves to the people, places or things we obsess about and then resist doing the rituals we feel will keep us safe. For thousands of years it has also been understood that living in the present moment makes life seem manageable and enjoyable (versus living in our thoughts about the future or memories of the past which can be fear-inducing and worrisome). Finally, it seems clear that at any point in time we can look at the elements of our life and see the them in a positive or negative light (glass half full or half empty) and, or take stock of either the positive of negative events and circumstances we have.

So here is an exercise which allows us to incorporate all three of those helpful strategies as we go through our day and encounter OCD triggers. When you run into a situation, person or thing which triggers your OCD:

(1) Stop and breath.

(2) Force your consciousness into the present moment. Be aware of exactly where you are in space and time. See, hear, smell and feel what is around you. Be here now.

(3) Notice the OCD part of your mind scanning for danger. Once you can clearly see it doing that - keep scanning but switch the scan to what you are grateful for in this place and time. (e.g. I am glad I have nice dishes, I am glad I have no trouble going to the bathroom, I am glad I have a telephone, etc.) Make sure to include the elements of whatever the obsession is about in your "gratitude list".

(4) Ask yourself, "Would the average person need to do the ritual the OCD is asking me to do?" The answer, of course, will be "no". Then refuse to do the ritual for 30 minutes. (What's the harm in waiting a little right?)

(5) Keep noticing what you are grateful for - anything and everything. Observe your anxiety and the strength of your desire to do the ritual you just refuse to do. By 30 minutes you will probably see the anxiety going down rather than up. So based on trend analysis it will eventually get to 0 right? So just continue on with your day. Oh, and you can now add this success to your gratitude list!

Copyright 2012 by Dr. Christian R. Komor (www.keiglobal.com)

CHAPTER THREE: SOME CONCLUDING THOUGHTS

We should add one caveat here. Conducting self-directed cognitive-behavioral therapy is very, very difficult without a guide, mentor, counselor, recovery buddy or some other type of individual who can assist. OCD tends to be self-perpetuating and it is extremely difficult to (1) separating from the obsessional thoughts and (2) staying consistent day after day with the ERP exercises. Like charging directly into enemy fire, recovery from OCD is a fairly straightforward process – but the courage it takes to get started and stay the course is often immense. Working with another makes the OCD less believable and keeps us on track.

As a side note, I like to point out that even if one gives in to an OC ritual it is still possible to make it a "win" by clearly acknowledging that one has had a "slip" and that the OC has won but that nothing real has been accomplished. A helpful statement here would be "I gave in to the OCD and its meaningless!" instead of "I protected myself (or accomplished something) by doing the OCD compulsion." Also, if one gives in to a ritual a healthy choice would be to find another similar challenge to do right away so that the OCD doesn't feel it has had a victory.

There are, of course, many other aspects to OCD recovery which are discussed in our article on ***Special Characteristics of OCD*** such as increased needs for reassurance or symmetry, neuropsychological and physical differences, etc. OCD recovery is not simply confronting rituals and compulsions, but undertaking this courageous task leads to all kinds of positive downstream effects such as reduced depression and increased feeling of self-sufficiency and spontaneity and free-will. Without ERP other important self-help measures (e.g. learning relaxation training, aerobic exercise, taking vacations) will likely eventually be overwhelmed by the compulsions and rituals. The freedom gained through ERP is a precious gift that only a recovering OCD sufferer can appreciate fully and the self-love which develops along the way is worth the effort.

APPENDIX: HELPFUL REMINDERS FOR DIFFICULT TIMES IN RECOVERY

Above all RELAX. Obsessive-Compulsive Spectrum disorders can be painful, but very, very seldom cause permanent physical or mental harm to the person – unless we cause harm to ourselves. Since OCD results from high anxiety it always makes sense to continually remind oneself to relax. This includes the caregivers and helper involved with the person.

Consider a temporary increase in medication, augmentation with another pharmacological agent, addition of an anti-anxiety agent (benzodiazepine, etc.) or
change in medication.

Reduce pressures related to life change by: Decreasing expectations, Following common routines, cancel a few activities, remind yourself that you control the speed and direction of treatment and slow things down if you need to.

Encourage a "Just be and don't think" approach on a continual basis. OCD lives in the mind. Redirect your attention to experiences versus thoughts.

Change the setting. Take a day off and go to the beach, grandparents, visiting friends, hiking, etc. Make note of positive changes experienced and take this experiential learning back to the regular routine.

Encourage yourself to feel and express your feelings (tears, anger, fear). Try and redirect attention away from:
- Ruminations and obsessive thoughts
- Verbal reassurance seeking
- Analyzing the OCD.

Focus on the positive progress and behaviors that you have achieved rather than the OCD.

Watch out for what is known as "thought-action-fusion". Remember that thoughts do not create reality. Stay out of magical thinking. Just because we step on a crack does not mean we are going to break our mother's back!

Finally, remember always to provide yourself with rewards for any and all progress. The road to recovery from OC-Spectrum and other compulsive disorders is rocky at best. Most of us take two steps forward and then one back. As we challenge ourselves to move forward on a daily basis we want to stay in our "growth" zone, but not our "panic" zone. Pushing too hard can undue progress we have already made.

OC-Spectrum disorders and other compulsive lifestyles have suffered through two extremes in professional approaches to treatment. After having initially be thought of as "neurotic" states resulting directly from poor parenting and the like, recent treatment efforts have focused almost exclusively on psychopharmacology and behavioral therapy designed to produce brain changes.

REFERENCES AND RECOMMENDED READINGS

Adams, P. *Obsessive Children*. New York: Penguin Books, 1973.
Alcoholics Anonymous (1976). New York: A.A. World Services
American Psychiatric Association (1987). *Diagnostic and Statistical Manual of Mental Disorders, Third Edition, Revised*. Washington, D.C.: American Psychiatric Association.
American Psychiatric Association. *Diagnostic and Statistical Manual of Mental Disorders, 4th Edition*. Washington: American Psychiatric Association, 1994.
Anonymous (1990). *The 12 Steps for Everyone*. Minneapolis: Compcare Publishers.
Azrin Nathan H., and Alan L. Peterson. "Behavior Therapy for Tourettes Syndrome and Tic Disorders." Chap. 16 in Donald J. Cohen et al., *Tourettes Syndrome and Tic Disorders: Clinical Understanding and Treatment*. New York: John Wiley, 1988.
Azrin Nathan H., and R. G. Nunn. *Habit Control in a Day*. New York: Simon and Schuster, 1977.
Azrin, Nathan H. *Habit Control in a Day*. New York: Simon and Schuster, 1977.
Azrin, Nathan H., and Alan L. Peterson. "Behavior Therapy for Tourettes Syndrome and Tic Disorders." Chap. 16 in Donald J. Cohen et. al., *Tourettes Syndrome and Tic Disorders: Clinical Understanding and Treatment*. New York: John Wiley, 1988.
Baer, Lee, and William E. Minichiello. "Behavior Therapy for Obsessive-Compulsive Disorder." In Burrows, G. D., R. Noyes, and M. Roth, eds., *Handbook of Anxiety*, vol. 4. Amsterdam: Elsevier Science, in press.
Baer, Lee, M.D. *Getting Control*. Boston: Little Brown and Company, 1991.
Barlow, D. H. and J. A. Cerny. *Psychological Treatment of Panic*. New York: Guilford Press, 1988.
Barlow, D. H. and M. Craske. *Mastery Of Your Anxiety and Pain*. Albany, New York: Graywind, 1989.
Bastiaans, J. (1968). "Psychoanalytic Investigations on the Psychic Aspects of Acute Myocardial Infarction". *Psychotherapy and Psychosomatics*. 1968, Vol 16(4.-5). Netherlands: University of Leyden.
Beattie, M. (1987). *Co-Dependent No More*. San Francisco: Harper/Hazelden.
Beattie, M. (1990). *A Co-Dependant's Guide to the 12 Steps*. New York: Prentice Hall.
Beattie, M. (1990). *The Language of Letting Go — Daily Meditations for Co-Dependents*. San Francisco: Harper and Row.
Beck, A. T., G. Emery, and R. L. Greenberg. *Anxiety Disorders and Phobias: A Cognitive Perspective*. New York: Basic Books.
Beck, J. S. *Cognitive Therapy: The Basics and Beyond*. New York: Guilford, 1995.
Beech, H. R. (Ed.). *Obsessional States*. London: Methuen, 1974.
Beech, H. R., and M. Vaughn. *Behavioral Treatment of Obsessional States*. New York: Wiley, 1978.
Benson, Herbert, and Miriam Z. Klipper. *The Relaxation Response*. New York: William Morrow, 1975.
Bland, R. C., H. Orn, and S. C. Newman, "Acta Psychiatric Scandinavia", 1988.
Bliss, J. "Sensory Experience of Gilles de la Tourette Syndrome." *Achieves of General Psychiatry* 37:1343-1347 (1980).

Bliss, J. "Sensory Experiences of Gilles de la Tourette Syndrome." *Archives of General Psychiatry*, 1980.

Bolton, D. *et. al.* "British Journal of Psychiatry", 1983.

Booth-Kewley, S. & Friedman, H.S. (1987). "Psychological Predictors of Heart Disease: A Quantitative Review". *Psychological Bulletin*. May 1987, Vol 101(3). University of California, Riverside.

Bradshaw, J. (1988). *Healing the Shame That Binds You*. Deerfield Beach, FL: Health Communications, Inc.

Brief, Arthur P., Rude, Dale E. & Rabinowitz, Samuel. (1983). "The Impact of Type A Behavior Pattern on Subjective Work Load and Depression". *Journal of Occupational Behavior*. April 1983, Vol 4(2). 157-164.

Brown, L.R. (1990). *The State of the World*. New York: W.W. Norton and Company.

Brownmiller, S. (1984). *Femininity*. New York: Fawcett.

Burke, Ronald J. (1985). "Career Orientations and Type A Behavior in Police Officers". Downsview, Canada.

Burrows, G. D., R. Noyes, and M. Roth. *Handbook of Anxiety, Volume 4*. Amsterdam: Elsevier Science, in press.

Calvocoressi, L., B. Lewis, M. Harris, S. J. Trufan, W. K. Goodman, C. J. McDougle, and L. H. Price. Family accommodations in obsessive-compulsive disorder. *American Journal of Psychiatry*, 1995.

Capacchione, L. (1979). *The Creative Journal: The Art of Finding Yourself*. Swallow Press/Ohio University Press.

Carnes, P. (1983). *Out of the Shadows*. Minneapolis: Compcare Publishers.

Carnes, P. (1989). *A Gentle Path Through The 12 Steps*. Minneapolis: Compcare Publishers.

Carnes, P. (1989). *Contrary to Love*. Minneapolis: Compcare Publishers.

Castine, J. (1989). *Recovery from Rescuing*. Deerfield Beach, FL: Health Communications, Inc.

Cermak, T.L. (1986). *Diagnosing and Treating Co-Dependence*. Minneapolis: Johnson Institute Books.

Clarke, J.I. & Dawson, C. (1989). *Growing Up Again: Parenting Ourselves and Our Children*. Minneapolis: Hazelden Educational Materials.

Conners, C., K. Wells, J. S. March, and C. Fiore. *Psychiatric Clinics of North America : Disruptive Behavior Disorders*. Philadelphia: Saunders, 1994.

Cousins, N. (1989). *Head First: The Biology of Hope*. New York: E.P. Dutton.

Crum, T. (1987). *The Magic of Conflict*. New York: Simon and Schuster, Inc.

D. Moreau, L. Mufson, M. M. Weissman, and G. L. Klerman. *Interpersonal Psychotherapy for Depressed Adolescents*. New York: Guilford Press, 1993.

Damos, Diane L. & Bloem, Kathryn A. (1985). "Type A Behavior Pattern, Multiple-Task Performance, and Subjective Estimation of Mental Workload". *Bulletin of the Psychonomic Society*. January 1985, Vol 23(1). 53-56. Arizona State University.

Damos, Diane L. (1985). "The Relation Between Type A Behavior Pattern, Pacing, and Subjective Workload Under Single- and Dual-Task Conditions". *Human Factors*. December 1985, Vol 27(6). 675-680. Los Angeles, California: University of Southern California.

Davis, M., McKay, M., & Eshelman, E.R. (1982). *The Relaxation and Stress Reduction Handbook*. Oakland, CA: New Harbinger Publications.

DeSaint-Exupery, A. (1943). *The Little Prince*. New York: Harcourt, Brace and World, Inc.

DeSilva, P. And S. Rachman. *Obsessive-Compulsive Disorder: The Facts*. Oxford: Oxford University Press, 1992.

Dornbush, M. and S. Pruit. *A Handbook for Individuals Involved in the Education of Students With Attention Deficit Disorders, Tourette Syndrome or Obsessive-Compulsive Disorder*. Duarte, CA: Hope Press, 1995.

Dougherty, S. (1989). "Analysis of a Selected Number of Female Workaholics". *Dissertation*. December 1989, Vol 50(6-A). Washington, D.C.: George Washington University.

Drosnin, Michael. *Citizen Hughes*. New York: Holt, Rinehart and Winston, 1985.

Ecker, R.E. (1985). *The Stress Myth*. Downers Grove, IL: InterVarsity Press.

Ellis, A. (1983). "My Philosophy of Work and Love." *Psychotherapy in Private Practice*. Spring 1983, Vol 1(1). New York, NY: Institute for Rational-Emotive Therapy.

Emmelkamp, P. M. G. *Phobic and obsessive-compulsive disorders: Theory, research and practice*. New York: Plenum Press, 1982.

Enhardt, D. and B. L. Baker. "Journal of Behavior Therapy and Experimental Psychiatry", 1990.

Erikson, E.H. (1963). *Childhood and Society*. New York: W.W. Norton & Company.

Eschholz, P. & Rosa, A. (1987). *Outlooks and Insights*. New York: St. Martin's Press, Inc.

Fassel, D. (1990) *Working Ourselves to Death - The High Cost of Workaholism and the Rewards of Recovery*. New York: Harper Collins.

Fassel, D. (1990) *Working Ourselves to Death: The High Cost of Workaholism and the Rewards of Recovery*. New York: Harper and Row.

Fields, R. (1984). *Chop Wood, Carry Water*. New York: Jeremy P. Tarcher.

Flament, M. F., A. Whitaker, J. L. Rapoport, M. Davies, C. Z. Berg, K. Kalikow, W. Sceery, and D. Shaffer. "Journal of American Academy Child Adolescent Psychiatry", 1988.

Forehand, R. L., and R. J. McMahon. *Helping the Noncompliant Child: A Clinician's Guide To Parent Training*. New York: Guilford Press, 1981.

Forgione, Albert and Frederic Bauer. *Fearless Flying: The Complete Program for Realized Air Travel*. Boston: Houghton Mifflin, 1980.

Fossum, M. (1989). *Catching Fire: Men's Renewal and Recovery Through Crisis*. Minneapolis: Hazelden Foundation.

Foster, Connie. *Funny, You Don't Look Crazy*. Dilligaf, Maine, 1993.

Foster, Connie. *Polly's Magic Games*. Dilligaf, Maine, 1993.

Francis, G., & Gragg, R. *Childhood obsessive-compulsive disorder*. Thousand Oaks, CA: Sage, 1996.

Freud, S. *The Standard Edition of the Complete Psychological Works of Sigmund Freud*. London: The Hogarth Press, 1925.

Friel, J. & Friel, L. (1988). *Adult Children: The Secrets of Dysfunctional Families*. Deerfield Beach, FL: Health Communications, Inc.

Friel, J. & Friel, L. (1990). *An Adult Child's Guide to What's "Normal"*. Deerfield Beach, FL: Health Communications, Inc.

Fritzler, B. K., J. E. Hecker, and M. C. Losee. *Behavior Research Therapy*, 1997.

Froggatt, Kirk L. & Cotton, John L. "The Impact of Type A Behavior Pattern on Overload-Induced Stress and Performance Attributions". *Journal of Management*. Spring 1987, Vol 13(1). 87-98.

Frost, R. O., and G. Steketee. *Obsessive-Compulsive Disorders: Theory and Management*. 3d ed. Chicago: Mosby Year Book Medical, 1998.

Fruehling, J. *Drug Treatment of OCD In Children and Adolescents*. Milford, CT: OC Foundation, 1997.

Furnham, Adrian F. (1990). "The Protestant Work Ethic and Type A Behavior: A Pilot Study. England.
Gibran, K. (1923). *The Prophet*. New York: Alfred A. Knopf Publishers.
Gillberg, C. "The Miller Memorial Lecture 1991". *Journal of Child Psychology and Psychiatry*, 1992.
Goodman, W. K., L. H. Price, S. A. Rasmussen, M. A. Riddle, and J. L. Rapoport. *Children's Yale-Brown Obsessive-Compulsive Scale.* New Haven: Clinical Neuroscience Research Unit, Health Center, 1991.
Gorman, Jack. *The Essential Guide to Psychiatric Drugs*. New York: St. Martin's Press, 1990.
Green, Robert, and Roger Pitman. "Tourette Syndrome and Obsessive-Compulsive Disorder: Clinical Relationships." Chap. 5 in Michael A. Jenike, Lee Baer, and William E. Minichiello, eds., *Obsessive-Compulsive Disorders: Theory and Management*, 2nd ed. Chicago: Year Book Medical Publishers, 1990.
Greist, J., J. Jefferson, I., Marks. *Anxiety and Its Treatment*. New York: Bantam, 1989.
Greist, John H. "Obsessive-Compulsive Disorder: A Guide." University of Wisconsin: Lithium Information Center, 1989.
Guidano, V. L., G. Liotti. *Cognitive Processes and Emotional Disorders*. New York: Guilford, 1983.
Guy, W. *ECDEU Assessment Manual for Psychopharmacology.* Washington D.C.: U. S. Department of Health, Education and Welfare, U. S. Government Printing Office, 1976.
Guyton, A.C. (1977). *Basic Human Psychology*. Second Edition, Philadelphia: Saunders.
Haas, R. (1989). "Workaholism: A Conceptual View and Development of a Measurement Instrument" *Dissertation*. November 1989, Vol 50(5-B). United States International University.
Halvorson, R. & Deilgar, V. (1989). *The 12 Steps — A Way Out: A Working Guide for Adult Children from Addictive and Other Dysfunctional Families.* Revised Edition, Recovery SD.
Helldorfer, M.C. (1987). "Church Professionals and Work Addiction". *Studies in Formative Spirituality*. May 1987, Vol 8(2). Middletown, CT: House of Affirmation, Consultation Center.
Hemfelt, Dr. R., Minirth, Dr. F., Meier, Dr. P. (1982). *We Are Driven — The Compulsive Behaviors America Applauds*. Nashville, TN: Thomas Nelson.
Hibbs, E. and P. Jensen. *Psychosocial Treatments For Child and Adolescent Disorders: Empirically Based Approaches*. Washington, D.C.: American Psychological Press, 1996.
Hiss, H., E. B. Foa, and M. J. Kozak. *Journal of Consulting and Clinical Psychology*, 1994.
Hollander, E., and D. J. Stein. Obsessive-Compulsive Disorders. New York: Marcel Dekker, Inc., 1997.
Hollander, J. (1990). *How to Make the World a Better Place*. New York: William Morrow.
Homer, J. (1985). "Worker Burnout: A Dynamic Model with Implications for Prevention and Control". *System Dynamics Review*. Summer, 1985, Vol 1(1). Los Angeles, CA: University of Southern California.
Hurrell, Joseph J. "Machine-Paced Work and the Type A Behavior Pattern". *Journal of Occupational Psychology*. March 1985, Vol 58(1). 15-25. Cincinnati, Ohio.
Hyman, B.M. and Pedrick, C. *The OCD Workbook*. Oakland, CA: New Harbinger, 1999.
Janas, C. (1987). "Seeking Magical Solutions, Exploring Addictions". *Medical Hypnoanalysis Journal*. March 1987, Vol 2(1).
Jenike, M. A.., L. Baer, and W. E. Minichiello. *Obsessive-Compulsive Disorder: Practical Medicine*. Chicago: Mosby, 1998.

Jenike, Michael A. "Somatic Treatments." Chap. 5 in Michael A. Jenike, Lee Baer, and William E. Minichiello, eds., *Obsessive-Compulsive Disorders: Theory and Management*, 1st ed. Littleton, Mass.: PSG Publishing, 1986.

Jenike, Michael, M.D. *Drug Treatment of OCD in Adults*. OCD Foundation, 1996.

Joffee, R. T., R. P. Swinson, and J. Regan. "American Journal of Psychiatry", 1988.

John-Roger & McWilliams, P. (1991). *Life 101*. New York: Bantam Books

Johnston, Hugh, M.D. *Obsessive-Compulsive Disorder in Children and Adolescents: A Guide*. Child Psycopharmacology Information Center, University of Wisconsin.

Joseph, B. (1985). "Process Communication Management: The Micro Chip of the O.D. World". *Organization Development Journal*. Fall 1985, Vol 3(3). Lakewood, OH: Taibi Kahler Associates.

Kelly, D. *Anxiety and Emotions: Physiologic basis and treatment*. Springfield, IL: Charles C. Thomas, 1980.

Kendall, P. C. *Child and Adolescent Therapy: Cognitive-Behavioral Procedures*. New York: Guildford Press, 1991.

Kendall, P.C. and S. M. Panichelli-Mindel. "Journal of Abnormal Child Psychology", 1995.

Keyes, R. (1991). *Timelock — How Life Got So Hectic and What You Can Do About It*. New York: Harper Collins.

Kinder, Dr. M. (1990) *Going Nowhere Fast — Step Off Life's Treadmills and Find Peace of Mind*. New York: Ballantine Books.

Kirmeyer, Sandra L. (1988). "Coping with Competing Demands: Interruption and the Type A Pattern". *Journal of Applied Psychology*. November 1988, Vol 73(4) 621-629. Columbia, Missouri: University of Missouri.

Komor, C. (1982). *The Relationship of Life Stress and Physiological Illness Among Undergraduate College Students*. San Diego: Christian Komor.

Komor, C. (1992). *The Power of Being — For People Who Do Too Much*. Grand Rapids, MI: Renegade House Productions.

Kritsberg, W. (1990). *Healing Together: A Guide to Intimacy and Recovery for Co-Dependent Couples*. Deerfield Beach, FL: Health Communications, Inc.

Kushnir, T. & Melamed, S. (1991). "Work-Load, Perceived Control and Psychological Distress in Type A/B Industrial Workers". *Journal of Organizational Behavior*. March 1991, Vol 12(2) 155-168. Ra'annana, Israel: Lowenstien Hospital.

LaoTzu (1944). *The Way of Life*. New York: Perigee Books.

Larrange, R. (1990). *Calling It A Day — Daily Meditations for Workaholics*. New York: Harper and Row.

Larson, E. (1985). *Stage Two Recovery: Life Beyond Addiction*. New York: W.W. Norton and Company.

Linehan, M. M. *Cognitive-behavioral treatment of borderline personality disorder*. New York: Guilford Press, 1993.

Lipinski, J., K. White, and S. Quay. *Antiobsessional effects of fluoxetine: An open trial*. Unpublished manuscript, 1988.

Livingston, Barbara, and Steven Rasmussen. "Learning to Live with Obsessive-Compulsive Disorder." New Haven, Conn.: OC Foundations, 1989.

Lochman, J., L. Lampron, T. Gemmer, and S. Harris. Innovations In Clinical Practice: A Source Book. Sarasota, FL: Professional Resource Exchange, 1987.

Machlowitz, M. (1979). "Determining the Effects of Workaholism". *Dissertation*. July 1979, Vol 40(1-B). Yale University.

Machlowitz, M. (1980). *Workaholics*. Reading, MA: Addison-Wesley.

March, J. S. (Ed.). *Anxiety Disorders In Children and Adolescents*. New York: Guilford Press, 1995.

Mathews, A. M., M. G. Gelder, and D. W. Johnston. *Agoraphobia: Nature and treatment.* New York: Guilford Press, 1981.

Matisiki, Edward N. M.A. *The Americans With Disabilities Act and Rehabilitation Act of 1973: Reasonable Accommodations for Employees with OCD.* OC Foundation, 1996.

Mavissakalian, M., S. M. Turner, and L. Michelson. (Eds.) *Obsessive-Compulsive Disorder: Psychological and Pharmacological Treatment.* New York: Plenum Press, 1985.

McGoldrick, M. & Gersen, R. (1985). *Genograms in Family Assessment*. New York: W.W. Norton and Company.

McKay, M., David, M., & Fanning, P. (1981). *Thoughts and Feelings: The Art of Cognitive Stress Intervention*. Oakland, CA: New Harbinger Publications.

Milkman, H. & Sunderwirth, S. (1987). *Craving for Ecstasy*. Lexington, MA: D.C. Heath and Company.

Miller, J. K. (1987). *Hope in the Fast Lane*. New York: Harper Collins.

Minirth, F., M.D.; Hawkins, D., Th.M.; Meier, P., M.D.; Flournoy, R., Ph.D. *How To Beat Burnout - Help for Men and Women*. Illinois: The Moody Bible Institute of Chicago.

Minirth, F.; Meier, P.; Wichern, F.; Brewer, B.; Skipper, S. (1981) *The Workaholic and His Family — An Inside Look*. Grand Rapids, MI: Baker Book House Company.

Nagy, S. & Davis, L.G. (1985). "Burnout: A Comparative Analysis of Personality and Environmental Variables". *Psychological Reports*. December 1985, Vol 57(3, pt 2). University of Alabama.

Napier, A.Y. (1988). *The Fragile Bond*. New York: Harper and Row.

Naughton, T. (1987). "A Conceptual View of Workaholism and Implications for Career Counseling and Research". *Career Development Quarterly*. March 1987, Vol 35(3). Detroit, MI: Wayne State University.

Newton, Tim J. & Keenan, Tony. (1990). "The Moderating Effect of the Type A Behavior Pattern and Locus of Control Upon the Relationship Between Change in Job Demands and Change in Psychological Strain". *Human Relations*. December 1990, Bol 43(12). 1229-1255. Scotland: University of Edinburgh.

Nezirogulu, Fugen, Ph.D. and Yaryura-Tobias, Jose, M.D. *Over and Over Again.* Lexington Books, 1991.

Orth-Gomer, Kristina & Unden, Anna Lena. (1990). "Type A Behavior, Social Support, and Coronary Risk: Interaction and Significance of Mortality in Cardiac Patients". *Psychosomatic Medicine*. January-February 1990, Vol 52(1). 59-772. Stockholm, Sweden.

Osbon, D.K. (1991). *Reflections On The Art of Living: A Joseph Campbell Companion*. New York: Harper Collins

Ottenberg, P. (1975). "The Physician's Disease: Success and Work Addiction". *Psychiatric Opinion*. April 1975, Vol 12(4). Philadelphia, PA: Private Practice.

Overbeck, T.J. (1976). "The Workaholic". *Psychology*. August 1979, Bol 13(3). University of Santa Clara Jesuit Community.

Pace, L.A. (1988). "Addictive Type-A Behavior Undermines Employee Involvement". *Personnel Journal*. June 1988, Vol 67(6). Webster, NY: Xerox Corporation.

Pato, M. T., and J. Zohar. (Eds.) *Current Treatments of Obsessive-Compulsive Disorder.* Washington, D.C.: American Psychiatric Press, 1990.

Paulley, J.W. (1975). "Cultural Influences on the Incidence and Pattern of Disease". *Psychotherapy and Psychosomatics*. 1975, Bol 26(1). England: Ipswich Hospital.

Paulus, T. (1972). *Hope for the Flowers*. New York: Paulist Press.

Penzer, W.N. (1984). "The Psychopathology of the Psychotherapist". *Psychotherapy in Private Practice*. Summer, 1984, Vol 2(2). Plantation, FL: Private Practice.

Peters, T.J. & Austin, N.K. (1989). *A Passion for Excellence*. Warner Books

Peterson, A.V. (1982). "Pathogram: A Visual Aid to Obtain Focus and Commitment". *Journal of Reality Therapy*. Fall 1982, Vol 2(1). Texas: Texas Technological University.

Pietropinto, A. (1986). "The Workaholic Spouse". *Medical Aspects of Human Sexuality*. May 1986, Vol 20(5). New York, NY: Cabrini Medical Center.

Rachman, S. J. and R. J. Hodgson. *Obsessions and compulsions*. Englewood Cliffs, NJ: Prentice Hall, 1980.

Rapoport, J. L. *Obsessive-Compulsive Disorder in Children and Adolescents*. Washington: American Psychiatric Press, 1989.

Rapoport, Judith L. *The Boy Who Couldn't Stop Washing*. New York: E.P. Dutton, 1989.

Rasmussen, Steven, and Jane Eisen. "Epidemiology and Clinical Features for Obsessive-Compulsive Disorders." Chap. 2 and 3 in Michael A. Jenike, Lee Baer, and William E. Minichiello, eds., *Obsessive-Compulsive Disorders: Theory and Management,* 2nd ed. Chicago: Year Book Medical Publishers, 1990.

Reed, G. F. *Obsessional experience and compulsive behavior*. Orlando, FL: Academic Press, 1985.

Riley, M. (1990). *Corporate Healing: Solutions to the Impact of the Addictive Personality in the Workplace*. Deerfield Beach, FL: Health Communications, Inc.

Robinson, B. (1989). *Work Addiction: Hidden Legacies of Adult Children*. Deerfield Beach, FL: Health Communications, Inc.

Robinson, B. (1990). *Soothing Moments: Daily Mediations for Fast-Track Living*. Deerfield Beach, FL: Health Communications, Inc.

Robinson, B. (1992). *Overdoing It: How to Slow Down and Take Care of Yourself*. Deerfield Beach, FL: Health Communications, Inc.

Rohrlich, J. (1980). *Work and Love: The Crucial Balance*.

Rohrlich, J. (1981). "The Dynamics of Work Addiction". *Israel Journal of Psychiatry and Related Sciences*. 1981, Vol 18(2). New York: Cornell University.

Schaef, A. & Fassel, D. (1988). *The Addictive Organization*. San Francisco: Harper and Row.

Schaef, A. (1986). *Women's Reality: An Emerging Female System in the White Male Society*. New York: Harper and Row.

Schaef, A. (1987). *When Society Becomes An Addict*. New York: Harper and Row.

Schor, J.B. (1991) *The Overworked American — The Unexpected Decline of Leisure*. New York: Basic Books

Schwartz, J. *Brain Lock*. New York: HarperCollins, 1996.

Seiler, R.E. (1984-85). "Dysfunctional Stress Among University Faculty". *Educational Research Quarterly*. 1984-85, Vol 9(2). Houston: University of Houston.

Shostrom, E. (1967). *Man, the Manipulator*. New York, Bantam Books.

Siegal, B. (1986). *Love, Medicine and Miracles*. New York: Harper and Row.

Sinetar, M. (1989). *Do What You Love: The Money Will Follow: Discover Your Right Livelihood*. Dell Trade Publishers.
Sorensen, Glorian & Jacobs, David R. (1987). "Relationships Among Type A Behavior, Employment Experiences, and Gender: The Minnesota Heart Survey". *Journal of Behavioral Medicine*. August 1987, Vol 10(4). 323-336. Worcester, Massachusetts: University of Massachusetts Medical School.
Sprankle, J. & Ebel, H. (1987). *The Workaholic Syndrome: Your Job Is Not Your Life* Walker and Company.
Spruell, G. (1987). "Work Fever". *Training and Development Journal*. January 1987, Vol 41(1). Alexandria, VA: American Society for Training and Development.
Steketee G., and N. A. Pruyn. *Obsessive-Compulsive Disorders: Theory, Research, and Treatment*. New York: Guilford, 1998.
Steketee, G. *Treatment of Obsessive-Compulsive Disorder*. New York: Guilford, 1993.
Steketee, G., and R. O. Frost. *Comprehensive Clinical Psychology: Vol. 6. Adults: Clinical Formulation & Treatment*. Oxford: Elsevier, 1998.
Steketee, Gail, Ph.D. and White, Kerrin, M.D. *When Once Is Not Enough*. Oakland, CA: New Harbinger Publications, 1990.
Steketee, Gail, Ph.D. *Treatment of OCD*. New York: The Guilford Press, 1993.
Subby, R.C. (1987). *Lost in the Shuffle*. Deerfield Beach, FL: Health Communications, Inc.
Subby, R.C. (1990). *Healing the Family*. Deerfield Beach, FL: Health Communications, Inc.
Swedo, S. E., and H. L. Leonard. *It's Not All in your Head*. New York: Harper Collins, 1996.
Swinson, R. P., M. M. Antony, S. Rachman, and M. A. Richter. *Obsessive-Compulsive Disorder: Theory, Research and Treatment*. New York: Guilford Press, 1998.
Thyer, B. A. "Behavior Modifications", 1991.
Tohei, K. (1980). *Ki In Daily Life*. Toyko, Ki No Kenkyukai H.Q.
Turner, S. M. and D. C. Beidel. *Treating Obsessive-Compulsive Disorder*. New York: Pergamon Press, 1988.
Van Noppen, B. L., M. T. Pato, and S. Rasmussen. *Learning to Live with OCD*. Milford, CT: OCD Foundation, 1993.
Walker, W. R., R. F. Freeman, and D. K. Christensen. *Behavior Therapy*, 1994.
Wegner, D. M. *White Bears and Other Unwanted Thoughts*. New York: Penguin, 1989.
Wells, K. *Anxiety Disorders in Children and Adolescents*. New York: Guilford Press, 1995.
Westman, M., Eden, D., & Shirom, A. (1985). "Job Stress, Cigarette Smoking and Cessation: The Conditioning Effects of Peer Support". *Social Science and Medicine*. 1985, Vol 20(6). Ramat-Aviv, Israel: Tel-Aviv University.
Wholey, D. (1988). *Becoming Your Own Parent*. New York: Doubleday.
Wilensky, A. *Passing for Normal: A Memoir of Compulsion*. New York: Broadway Books, 2000
Williams, P. (1987). *Remember Your Essence*. New York: Harmony Books.
Winokur, J. (1989). *Zen To Go*. New York: Penguin Books.
Woititz, J.G. (1983). *Adult children of Alcoholics*. Deerfield Beach, FL: Health Communications, Inc.
Woititz, J.G. (1985). *Struggle for Intimacy*. Deerfield Beach, FL: Health Communications, Inc.
Woititz, J.G. (1987). *Home Away From Home: The Art of Self-Sabatoge*. Deerfield Beach, FL: Health Communications, Inc.
Wolpe, J. *Psychotherapy by reciprocal inhibition*. Stanford, CA Stanford University Press, 1958.

Woodside, M. (1986). *Children of Alcoholics On the Job.*

World Health Organization. *ICD-10 International Statistical Classification of Disease and Related Health Problems.* Tenth Revision. Geneva: WHO, 1992.

Yaryura-Tobias, J. A. and F. Neziroglu. Biobehavioral Treatment of Obsessive-Compulsive Disorders. New York: W. W. Norton & Co., 1997.

Zohar, J., T. Insel, and S. Rasmussen. (Eds.) *The Psychobiology of Obsessive-Compulsive Disorder.* New York: Springer, 1991.

Made in the USA
Lexington, KY
22 October 2012